WHERE
FAITH
&
CULTURE
MEET

PARTICIPANT'S GUIDE

WHERE
FAITH
&
CULTURE
MEET

INTERSECT

SIX SESSIONS ON HOW YOU CAN ENGAGE YOUR CULTURE

CONNECT

ANDY CROUCH
EDITORIAL DIRECTOR

Written by COLLIN HANSEN and MARK GALLI

ZONDERVAN®

ZONDERVAN.com/
AUTHORTRACKER
follow your favorite authors

CHRISTIANITYTODAY
INTERNATIONAL

www.christianvisionproject.com

Where Faith and Culture Meet Participant's Guide
Copyright © 2007 by Christianity Today International

Requests for information should be addressed to:

Zondervan, *Grand Rapids, Michigan 49530*

ISBN-10: 0-310-28096-6
ISBN-13: 978-0-310-28096-5

Interior design by Mark Sheeres

Printed in the United States of America

08 09 10 11 12 • 23 22 21 20 19 18 17 16 15 14 13 12 11 10 9 8 7 6 5 4 3 2

used - Well Class: Feb/March 2010 (Student sheets created)

CONTENTS

INTRODUCTION

Welcome to *Where Faith and Culture Meet*! This resource was born out of the prayers and passions of people who love the body of Christ and want to see the church flourish in our culture. As your group watches the accompanying DVD, you will be inspired by five stories of people who have responded to God's call to serve him in bold ways. As you engage in Bible study and discussion, you will discover God's challenge to all of us—to minister to our culture—and what that means for you.

It is our prayer that *Where Faith and Culture Meet* will change your life and the lives of your group members, just as it has transformed the lives of those of us who have enjoyed working on the Christian Vision Project (for more information, see www.christianvisionproject. com). May the Holy Spirit work in and through your group as you challenge each other to see where faith and culture meet.

SESSION 1

BEGIN

1 Peter 2:9–17

But you are a chosen people, a royal priesthood, a holy nation, a people belonging to God, that you may declare the praises of him who called you out of darkness into his wonderful light.

1 Peter 2:9

KEY ISSUE

God calls the church to be a counterculture for the common good.

Culture is how we understand the world around us. It's about language and values, the common understanding of beauty, the media we share, and it's even about coffee. A coffee shop is a "place where you meet your friends, where you bring your kids. It's a place where people read and write," Andy Crouch says. "Food, friendships, creativity, architecture, politics, commerce—it's all here." In other words, it's culture.

Culture is a creation of people made in God's image. And, as Crouch explains, it's also the scene of rebellion against God. These created people break God's law in every way in every place. Yet God calls his people to live counter to the culture, to live in God's counterculture. It's called the church. And the most distinctively countercultural activity of that community is worship, where we honor not the false idols of this world (money, sex, and power mostly) but the Lord of

Lords. Worship is where heaven meets earth so that our eyes can see beyond the horizon of history and death.

After God calls us into this counterculture, he begins transforming us. He does this so we, like Abraham, may become a blessing to the world. He calls us not to be a counterculture for our own salvation, but a counterculture for the common good. We tend what's beautiful. We mend what's broken. Using the means provided us by God, we show people where to find forgiveness of sins, the resurrection of the body, and the life everlasting.

OPENING (1 min.)

It's often said that Christians are to live in this world but not of it. This is not an easy or comfortable tension. The winds of culture sometimes blow at the church's back, urging Christians toward love and good deeds. Yet sometimes the winds shift and fly right in the face of God's people. No matter the situation, God's calling remains the same—for his church to be a counterculture for the common good.

DVD TEACHING AND DISCUSSION (20 min.)

DVD Notes

Culture is . . .

The darker story . . .

Jesus and culture . . .

Asking the questions . . .

DVD Group Discussion

1 What is culture, according to Andy Crouch?

2 What is a counterculture? Name a few historical countercultures.

3 What is a counterculture for the common good?

"I think every Christian effort to contribute to culture, to participate in culture, should begin by understanding that Jesus is already present, working in *every* human culture." *Andy Crouch*

4 We belong to a variety of overlapping cultures — generation, nation, local community, common interests, and so on. Describe the cultures you find yourself in.

5 What makes Christians countercultural?

6 Where do you see the hand of God in your culture?

BIBLE EXPLORATION AND APPLICATION
(15–20 min.)

Read 1 Peter 2:9–17 together.

1 How does Peter describe the church? How is this different from any other human institution?

2 How should Christians live, according to Peter? What is the point of doing "good deeds"?

3 What, according to Peter, should be the Christian's relationship to cultural institutions?

4 Are Christians already a counterculture? Or do they need to become a counterculture? Explain your answer.

5 What happens when Christians do not live distinct from culture?

6 How does God's counterculture attract outsiders?

7 What is broken about your church—your counterculture—that prevents it from working more effectively for the common good?

8 How does your church creatively engage its culture?

GROUP ACTIVITY (8–10 min.)

If you have enough time, we recommend that you choose one of these group experiences:

Optional Activity #1

Watch the last part of the "Begin" segment on the DVD, in which Ken Fong and Lauren Winner comment about the session topic. Discuss the following questions:

1 What comment was most interesting/revealing/helpful to you? Why?

2 What comment did you most disagree with? Why?

3 What, if any, further application is there for you or your church?

"Because human beings are made in the image of God, culture can be amazing. It can be beautiful. It can be wonderful."

Andy Crouch

Optional Activity #2

Distribute Martin Luther King Jr.'s "Letter from Birmingham Jail" (see: http://almaz.com/nobel/peace/MLK-jail.html). Select a portion for your group to read during your time together. Discuss how the civil rights movement in the United States acted as a counterculture for the common good. How does the letter challenge the church to live up to its countercultural calling?

CLOSING (1 min.)

The ultimate aim of this experience is to prompt thinking about what we can do together tomorrow, this year, and over the next ten years to create a counterculture for the common good. Pray that God will work in the hearts of your group to mindfully live distinct from the culture, yet for the benefit of all your neighbors.

TO DO ON YOUR OWN

To better understand your culture, keep a journal of messages you hear in media, from friends at work or school, and from your church's pulpit. Consider how these messages weave a cultural pattern but also how they might contradict each other.

DWELL

John 1:1–4, 14; Philippians 2:5–8; Hebrews 2:14–18

The Word became flesh and made his dwelling among us.

John 1:14

KEY ISSUE

When we live closely with others, we find new opportunities to minister.

Surrounded by the hustle and bustle of New York City, Makoto Fujimura's studio is a refuge of contemplation and beauty. Yet on September 11, 2001, there was no refuge from the chaos. Stranded in the subway when the first World Trade Center tower collapsed, Mako (MAH-ko) scrambled to reach his wife and children. The smoke disoriented him, but eventually the whole family was reunited and arrived home safely. Even now he struggles to comprehend the experence.

Mako did not envision such a traumatic day when in 1997 he moved his family from New Jersey to Manhattan. Mako had responded to a challenge from his pastor to live among the city's artists, to reflect the love of Christ within a community that seems to care little for the things of God. Moving to his new neighborhood and church helped Mako connect with the people there—especially his fellow artists. Thus, when 9/11 occurred, he was able to minister in unprecedented ways. His studio hosted art exhibits, poetry readings, and other events to create an "oasis of dialogue" amid a coping city, ultimately in order to point people to the grace and mercy of Christ.

OPENING (1 min.)

Just as "the Word became flesh and made his dwelling among us" (John 1:14), so we are called to "move in" and dwell more fully in our neighborhoods, workplaces, and schools so that we can minister to others in Christ's name. For some—like Mako Fujimura in the DVD you are about to see—it means making a literal move. For others, it will mean thinking creatively about getting more involved in the lives of the people and community they want to serve.

DVD TEACHING AND DISCUSSION (20 min.)

DVD Notes

Art is . . .

Arena of grace . . .

"Art is all about being authentic and being honest before God about my own conditions, things that I struggle with." *Makoto Fujimura*

Living incarnationally . . .

September 11 . . .

An oasis of dialogue . . .

DVD Group Discussion

1 What does painting signify for Mako regarding his relationship with Christ?

2 What spiritual themes do art critics identify in Mako's painting?

3 How did moving to New York City enhance Mako's ability to minister to artists?

4 What risks do you think Mako took when he moved his family into a new neighborhood?

5 Immediately after September 11, what difference did it make that Mako was already living in New York City?

6 Mako makes paint by crushing pigment, which is referred to in the DVD as a metaphor for God's work of redemption. Is this a meaningful metaphor to you? Why or why not?

BIBLE EXPLORATION AND APPLICATION
(15 – 20 min.)

Read the following Bible passages together: John 1:1 – 4, 14; Philippians 2:5 – 8; and Hebrews 2:14 – 18.

1 Examine the different words/metaphors that each passage uses to describe the theological doctrine we call the incarnation. What do they all have in common? What are the significant differences?

2 If you were to ask each writer, "Why did God become human?" what would each say?

3 God could have chosen an infinite number of ways to love and redeem his creation. Why do you think he chose this way?

4 Thinking back to the DVD presentation, how is Mako's move to New York City like Christ's incarnation? How is it different?

5 In what ways, before and after 9/11, did Mako "share in the sufferings" of his community?

"We are a minority culture with a voice that can put a framework to the entire culture."

Makoto Fujimura

6 What are some of the "sufferings" of your community that you think your church is called to share in?

7 In what ways could your church "move in" more deeply in your community? How can it become an even deeper part of its life? What might be the next step(s) in making this happen?

GROUP ACTIVITY (8 – 10 min.)

If you have enough time, we recommend that you choose one of these group experiences:

Optional Activity #1

Watch the last part of the "Dwell" segment on the DVD, in which Tim Keller and Brenda Salter McNeil comment about the session topic. Discuss the following questions:

1 What comment was most interesting/revealing/helpful to you? Why?

2 What comment did you most disagree with? Why?

3 What, if any, further application is there for you or your church?

Optional Activity #2

Turn to Timothy J. Keller's Christian Vision Project article, "A New Kind of Urban Christian," on pages 59–63 of the Appendix and select a portion for your group to read during your time together. Divide the group among those who agree and those who disagree with Keller's argument that more Christians should move to the cities, because those places influence the larger culture. Encourage each side to debate using the DVD, article, and their experience. Give them a few minutes to brainstorm talking points and to designate a leader to make the case.

CLOSING (1 min.)

Read Philippians 2:5–11. Pray together that God would give your church wisdom to "move in" more deeply to the community where, by God's providence, it finds itself, and to serve it in humble and creative ways.

TO DO ON YOUR OWN

■ Meditate on John 1:1–4, 14; Philippians 2:5–8; or Hebrews 2:14–18. Journal about the communities where you've lived and ministered. In what ways did you incarnate yourself there? What more might you have done? What difference did your presence make, as far as you can tell? What can you learn from this experience? In what ways are you personally called to "move in" more deeply in your work, home, or school? What would you hope God would accomplish through you in this way?

- If your group did not select Optional Activity #2, take some time to read Timothy J. Keller's Christian Vision Project article, "A New Kind of Urban Christian" (pages 59–63) on your own during the week.

SESSION 3

UNITE

Luke 10:1–9

He told them, "The harvest is plentiful, but the workers are few. Ask the Lord of the harvest, therefore, to send out workers into his harvest field."

Luke 10:2

KEY ISSUE

We serve more effectively and joyfully when we serve together.

Frank Sabo took the first step when he agreed to drive the youth van. Little did he know how that little step would lead his whole family to commit to tutoring immigrant children. God captured his heart for service once he saw the need.

Julie Sawyer's family took their service one step further. They moved into an apartment complex where many immigrants lived. Now the community's concerns have become her family's concerns. Living among the needs keeps Julie's heart tender for serving her neighbors.

Both Frank and Julie quickly learned that empathy alone could not sustain the demanding call to serve strangers selflessly. They drew strength from a natural source—their close-knit families. Tutoring together with their spouses and children, Frank and Julie can better serve the kids. At the same time, their families' bonds grow even stronger.

It's the way God planned for his church to work. First, love of God leads us to care for others. Then others encourage us to persevere as we work together—often as families, as the DVD segment "Unite" shows, but also with others in the family we call the church. Finally, the work strengthens the very bonds that enabled us to serve in the first place.

OPENING (1 min.)

The Sabo and Sawyer families would certainly agree, "It's better to give than receive." Watch how God opened their eyes to the needs of their community and inspired them to meet those needs together.

DVD TEACHING AND DISCUSSION (20 min.)

DVD Notes

Needs in the suburbs . . .

Families serving together . . .

Moving in . . .

Making a kingdom impact together ...

DVD Group Discussion

1 How did Frank Sabo get started with tutoring kids in the nearby apartments?

2 What risks did the Sawyers take moving into the apartment complex?

3 What preserves Julie Sawyer's compassion for her neighbors? Why?

4 What difference does it make that the Sabo and Sawyer families serve *together*?

5 How does Perimeter Church encourage service based on the congregation's strengths?

BIBLE EXPLORATION AND APPLICATION

(15 – 20 min.)

Read Luke 10:1 – 9 together.

1 Why, according to this passage, does Jesus send out the disciples two by two? What other New Testament examples suggest that serving together is the norm?

2 What aspects of Jesus' commands to his disciples surprise you?

3 Thinking back to the DVD presentation, what for the Sabos and Sawyers is the Luke 10:17 experience — what for them is the joy of ministry?

> "To be truly countercultural, the church must first receive and then witness to Peter's claim in Acts 2:39: 'The promise is for you and your children and for all who are far off — for all whom the Lord our God will call.' The promise is not only for us, but also for our children."
>
> *Michael S. Horton*

4 What are other reasons we should serve with others besides the one mentioned in Luke 10?

5 Jesus is acutely aware of human nature, and he knows that when we serve with others, there will be disagreements, irritations, personality clashes, even arguments. What, if anything, is to be gained from such "negative" experiences?

6 Has your family served together in some way? Tell the group about the experience, both the challenges and the rewards.

7 If you don't have family near you, what group provides you an opportunity to serve with others?

8 Frank Sabo's call to ministry started when he agreed to drive the van. What first step might allow your nuclear family or church group to better discern how God wants you to serve?

GROUP ACTIVITY (8 – 10 min.)

If you have enough time, we recommend that you choose one of these group experiences:

Optional Activity #1

Watch the last part of the "Unite" segment on the DVD, in which Lauren Winner, Brenda Salter McNeil, and James Meeks comment about the session topic. Discuss the following questions:

1 What comment was most interesting/revealing/helpful to you? Why?

2 What comment did you most disagree with? Why?

3 What, if any, further application is there for you or your church?

> "The 'pumped-up' teens in our youth groups today are often tomorrow's skeptics and burnouts. They don't need more hip Christian slogans, T-shirts, and other subcultural distractions, but the means of grace for maturing into coheirs with Christ."
>
> *Michael S. Horton*

Optional Activity #2

Organize a role play. Designate one person as a parent and the other as a teenage son or daughter. The parent has decided the family will minister together on Sunday afternoons at a community center in a nearby neighborhood. That neighborhood is much different from the family's, and the teen doesn't want to go. How will the parent persuade the child to help? (You can divide the whole group into pairs, or just designate two people to act on behalf of the whole group.)

CLOSING (1 min.)

Pray that God would reveal to each person in the group where they might serve God, and with whom they should serve.

TO DO ON YOUR OWN

- In your journal or prayer time, consider your networks—church, family, work, neighborhood, school, leisure activities, and so on. What opportunities do you have to serve with these groups? What about your *Where Faith and Culture Meet* study group? Ask God to show your group how they can spur one another on to serve him together.

- Take some time during the upcoming week to read and reflect on Michael S. Horton's article, "How the Kingdom Comes" (pages 65 – 70).

RECONCILE

Galatians 3:28; Revelation 7:9 – 17

There is neither Jew nor Greek, slave nor free, male nor female, for you are all one in Christ Jesus.

Galatians 3:28

KEY ISSUE

God wants to heal our racial and ethnic divisions, especially in and through his church.

Pain can linger for decades in an individual or culture, long after those who inflicted the pain have forgotten. That's the case on Vancouver Island, British Columbia. Nearby Kuper Island was the longtime home of an infamous residential school where young First Nations children learned the ways of Western culture away from their native families.

Now nothing remains of the school but rubble. But the legacy endures. The stone blocks remind Vancouver Island's indigenous population that all the surrounding land once belonged to them, until white settlers squatted and never left. The newly dominant culture marginalized the First Nations people. Even today, poverty and low expectations plague them.

Unfortunately, churches not only turned a blind eye to Canadian authorities as they yanked First Nations children from their parents.

They were actually agents of the government's indoctrination efforts. The churches thought they were helping the children by giving them a Western education, which likely included Christian teaching. What they couldn't see is evident in retrospect—how the school sapped the spirit of the First Nations people.

Mark Buchanan's church decided that this history, and the current ethnic divisions between white and First Nations people, needed to be addressed. They began by simply trying to understand what went wrong and why. They've continued with slow, humble steps to incarnate the biblical reality that there is no Jew nor Greek, no white nor First Nations, but all of us are one in Christ.

OPENING (1 min.)

With our perspective so limited, it's easy to lose track of how God is moving in other peoples and cultures. We can even unintentionally work against God if ignorance blinds us to the full consequences of our actions. That's part of the story on Vancouver Island, where the First Nations people have suffered the "good intentions" of British pioneers and the church. Now some Christian leaders are prodding the church to open its eyes to this legacy and seek racial reconciliation.

DVD TEACHING AND DISCUSSION (20 min.)

DVD Notes

Heaven is described as . . .

The history of the Cowichan lands and Kuper Island . . .

The responsibility of the church ...

True reconciliation ...

Standing up to make it right ...

DVD Group Discussion

1 What is Pastor Mark Buchanan's reason for having his church think about racial and ethnic issues?

2 What does the site of the residential school symbolize to the native tribes?

"One of the greatest sins ... against heaven is how racially segregated our churches are."

Mark Buchanan

3 What is Graham Bruce doing to redeem the church's legacy?

4 Does the church built on stolen land have any special obligation to reconcile with the First Nations people? If so, what should they do about the land?

5 Do you feel guilty about wrongs committed by your ancestors? Why or why not?

BIBLE EXPLORATION AND APPLICATION
(15–20 min.)

Read Revelation 7:9–17 together.

1 What are some characteristics of heaven as described here?

2 What difference does it make that people from every nation, tribe, people, and language will worship God in heaven? Why do you suppose the Bible highlights the racial and ethnic makeup of heaven (see also Rev. 21:24)?

3 Read Galatians 3:28. What does this verse suggest about the current reality of racial reconciliation?

4 Why does the DVD segment spend so much time on speaking about the past? What good does that do?

5 How exactly does uncovering past injustices help us to more fully reconcile today?

6 Does the portrait of diversity described by Revelation 7 excite you? Why or why not?

"My hope is that the church in America will embrace its ethnic diversity as a vital part of humanity that can be redeemed for the purposes of God. If we do, we can offer something special to the wider world."

Orlando Crespo

7 Who are the unique ethnic and racial groups in your community? How might they experience injustice at the hands of the dominant culture? Have local churches played any role in that injustice?

8 What might be one small step your church could take to realize racial or ethnic reconciliation in your community?

GROUP ACTIVITY (8–10 minutes)

If you have time, we recommend that you choose one of these group experiences:

Optional Activity #1

Watch the last couple minutes of the "Reconcile" segment on the DVD for analysis from Lauren Winner, Amy Laura Hall, and Brenda Salter McNeil. Then ask the group the following questions:

1 What prevents the church from being more racially integrated?

2 What makes us susceptible to becoming condescending to people of other races and ethnicities?

3 Does your community have problems everyone observes but few talk about? If so, what are they?

4 Other than race, what characteristics divide the people of your community?

5 Who do you think live out the most helpful examples of racial and ethnic reconciliation, in your community or elsewhere?

Optional Activity #2

Watch Martin Luther King Jr.'s "I Have a Dream" speech (go to http://video.google.com/ and search for "I Have a Dream"). What are his Christian arguments for racial justice? How has American society fulfilled and/or failed his vision?

CLOSING (1 min.)

Note all the ethnic and racial groups in your community. Have different people in the group pray for one group in particular. Close by joining hands and saying together the Lord's Prayer, "*Our* Father ..."

TO DO ON YOUR OWN

■ This week take notice of the types of people you spend time with at work, church, school, or elsewhere. Pray for opportunities to meet or talk with someone of a different race or ethnicity.

■ Take some time during the upcoming week to read and reflect on Orlando Crespo's article "Our Transnational Anthem" (pages 71–76).

INVEST

2 Timothy 1:1 – 7; 2:1 – 7; 4:9 – 13, 21a

To Timothy, my dear son. . . .

2 Timothy 1:2

KEY ISSUE

Transforming entire communities begins when we give ourselves to people, one by one.

Rudy Carrasco didn't need to come back to his neighborhood. That's why people go to Stanford, so they can make a better life for themselves elsewhere. Stanford grads definitely don't end up in the kind of neighborhoods Carrasco grew up in, beset by drug deals, prostitution, and gang violence. Besides, Carrasco endured plenty of bad memories back home. That's where his mother died, where his sister had to turn down an Ivy League education to take care of her young siblings.

But Carrasco did come back. More important, he stayed, and he's been working with people one by one to help transform the broken community. The chief example in the DVD "Invest" is the long-term and very personal commitment he made to Jamaal Johnson. Now we see that Jamaal has committed himself to serving other people in the same way.

This whole process — caring for people one by one — is modeled especially in Paul's relationship with Timothy. It stands at the core of our calling to love as Christ loves us, individually and lastingly.

OPENING (1 min.)

There is nothing glamorous about Rudy Carrasco's work. The job demands uncommon patience and persistence, and promises no results. Yet no less a commitment can really change a person or community.

DVD TEACHING AND DISCUSSION (20 min.)

DVD Notes

The neighborhood ...

God cares about cities ...

Jamaal's story ...

Harambee changes things ...

"I've found that it's relatively easy to raise a voice in protest, but unfathomably hard to invest in a life."

Rodolpho Carrasco

DVD Group Discussion

1 What problems do people in northwest Pasadena endure?

2 How did the biblical story of Jericho inspire Rudy?

3 What bonded Jamaal and Rudy?

4 How does Jamaal plan to return the grace extended to him by Rudy?

5 What do you think it means to people in Pasadena that Rudy returned there after Stanford?

6 What do you imagine are some of the obstacles to Rudy's work?

BIBLE EXPLORATION AND APPLICATION

(15–20 min.)

Read 2 Timothy 1:1–7; 2:1–7; 4:9–13, 21a together.

1 List the various ways these verses suggest a very personal bond between Paul and Timothy.

2 What exactly is the nature of their relationship? What is Paul hoping to accomplish by investing himself in Timothy?

3 What hints are there in the verses that Paul has invested in Timothy for some time?

4 Thinking back to the DVD presentation, how does Rudy model Paul's ministry style? What are the key characteristics of Paul and Rudy's ministry of investing in others, one by one?

5 How do we prevent ministry programs, especially those designed to help people, from swallowing up or overshadowing these very people?

6 What are the risks and challenges of investing in individual lives? What might be the rewards?

7 What keeps you from investing more in another individual?

8 Whom do you consider your mother or father in the faith? Describe how that person invested in you. What can you learn from your own experiences about investing in others?

"When did you last spend time with a poor person, an at-risk individual, or someone in need? When was the last time you were close to them for an extended period? I ask, because that's what Jesus did."   *Rodolpho Carrasco*

GROUP ACTIVITY (8–10 min.)

If you have enough time, we recommend that you choose one of these group experiences:

Optional Activity #1

Watch the rest of the "Invest" DVD segment for analysis from Tim Keller, Lauren Winner, and Amy Laura Hall. Discuss the following questions:

1 As he drives past beautiful mansions, Rudy describes the mix of privilege and poverty in Pasadena. What are the greatest needs in your community?

2 How long do you plan to stay in your community? Would you consider staying longer if you and your church had a vision for how to bring about lasting change?

3 Are you a better host or guest? Explain.

4 What encourages you to endure while serving others?

5 What do you appreciate about the churches and other ministries serving your community? Give specifics, if possible.

Optional Activity #2

Turn to Mick Dumke's article "Meeks Preaches Church Activism" about Salem Baptist Church on Chicago's South Side (pages 77–78 of the Appendix). Use this article as a case study of a church that has persisted to change its neighborhood. Discuss Salem Baptist Church and how your church could be a change agent in your community.

CLOSING (1 min.)

Lead the group in silent meditation, asking them to spend a few moments listening to the Spirit's prompting about whom they might invest their lives in even more. Then close in prayer.

TO DO ON YOUR OWN

- "When did you last spend time with a poor person, an at-risk individual, or someone in need?" Rudy asks in his Christian Vision Project article, "Habits of Highly Effective Justice Workers." As an individual or, better yet, as a family or small group, choose an activity to serve and spend time with people in need. Consider a local community center, homeless/abuse shelter, pregnancy crisis center, or food bank. Afterward, take time to consider what you learned from the outing.

- Take some time this week to read and reflect on Rudy Carrasco's article, "Habits of Highly Effective Justice Workers" (pages 79–84).

ABIDE

Colossians 3:12 – 17; 4:2 – 4; Matthew 6:2, 5, 16

Devote yourselves to prayer, being watchful and thankful.

Colossians 4:2

KEY ISSUE

Spiritual disciplines help us to abide in Christ so we can serve faithfully.

Frederica Mathewes-Green is a wide-ranging author whose work has appeared in such diverse publications as the *Washington Post*, the *Los Angeles Times*, *First Things*, *Books and Culture*, *Touchstone*, the *Wall Street Journal*, and *Christianity Today*. She has published seven books and more than six hundred articles and has spoken at numerous colleges and universities, among them Yale, Harvard, Princeton, Wellesley, Cornell, Calvin, Baylor, and Westmont, as well as the Family Research Council and the National Right to Life Committee.

Mathewes-Green doesn't start a day before praying. Well, after she's started her tea, at least. She prays and thinks through the rest of the day. "Spiritual disciplines equip us to be healed people who can then go out and begin to change our culture no matter where we are, how small or large our context," she says. "We can be the presence of Christ—the fragrance of Christ—in every place, and begin to change our world."

Jesus has given Mathewes-Green tremendous gifts to understand the culture. She has identified a common loneliness we try to hide by consuming goods—clothes, cars, homes, and so on. Yet no one and no thing can ever fill the hole in our hearts except God, she teaches. He has designed us to live in communion with him and in community with others.

If she's going to help Christians fight cultural captivity, Mathewes-Green knows she needs the help of spiritual disciplines. Her practice of the spiritual disciplines helps her to be active in the culture and to have an evangelical spirit that seeks to engage people with the love of Jesus Christ. Other than prayer and contemplation, she also fasts and worships in community. By abiding in Christ in these ways, she becomes equipped to do the work God wants her to do in the world.

In this session we focus on the spiritual disciplines that undergird a life of service in the culture. We've seen a variety of ways to engage the culture—to live out God's counterculture for the common good. But to attempt that without first connecting with God and drawing on his strength will be an exercise in futility. Through God's love and strength, it will be a joy.

OPENING (1 min.)

Frederica Mathewes-Green is an accomplished writer and speaker. But she recognizes that anything she has to offer others comes from Christ working through her. God cultivates that blessing as she dwells in Christ through spiritual disciplines.

DVD TEACHING AND DISCUSSION (20 min.)

DVD Notes

Icons: a serious question . . .

Loneliness and dislocation ...

Why doesn't the church *do* something?

The Jesus Prayer ...

The presence of the Lord ...

DVD Group Discussion

1 According to Mathewes-Green, how do the various spiritual disciplines help us minister to others?

2 What emotion does Mathewes-Green say typifies her audiences? Do you perceive the same longing?

3 How does Mathewes-Green say God will change the world?

4 What are the dangers of overabundance?

5 Has something good, like family, become an idol for you? If so, explain.

6 How do you "encounter Jesus"?

"Spiritual disciplines equip us to be healed people who can go out and begin to change our culture."

Frederica Mathewes-Green

BIBLE EXPLORATION AND APPLICATION

(15 – 20 min.)

Read Colossians 3:12 – 17; 4:2 – 4 and Matthew 6:2, 5, and 16 together.

1 In the Matthew passage, Jesus gave the disciples instructions about how they should give, pray, and fast. What did he *assume* about his disciples?

2 In the Colossians passages, what are the two spiritual disciplines Paul encouraged?

3 Why did Paul suggest these disciplines in the middle of a series of exhortations about how to do ministry and how to live together as a church? What was he saying by mixing things up like this?

4 Spiritual disciplines are sometimes called spiritual exercises, meant to strengthen us as do physical exercises. There are many types of spiritual disciplines, but talk about how each of the spiritual disciplines mentioned in these passages — Bible reading, prayer, giving, and fasting — strengthen us.

5 Which spiritual discipline most helps you sense God's presence, most helps you abide in Christ? Explain.

6 Give a recent example of how spiritual discipline strengthened you for service to others.

7 What is the spiritual discipline you would most like to grow in? Why?

8 What obstacles get in the way of our consistent practice of spiritual disciplines? What strategies have you successfully used to overcome these obstacles?

GROUP ACTIVITY (8 – 10 min.)

If you have enough time, we recommend that you choose one of these group experiences:

Optional Activity #1

Watch the last part of the "Abide" segment on the DVD, in which James Meeks, Ken Fong, and Lauren Winner comment about the session topic. Discuss the following questions:

1 What comment was most interesting/revealing/helpful to you? Why?

2 What comment did you most disagree with? Why?

3 What, if any, further application is there for you or your church?

Optional Activity #2

Mathewes-Green talks about loneliness and how our culture plugs the hole with indulgence—food, clothing, sex, cars, and the like. Ask the group to count the number of labels and brand names they see in the room, especially on clothes or accessories. Discuss what the labels we wear tell about us. What labels make you feel better about yourself? What are we told to think about labels? How do you define yourself? Do your labels conflict with this definition?

"We can be the presence of Christ—the fragrance of Christ—in every place."

Frederica Mathewes-Green

CLOSING ^(1 min.)

Pray for each person briefly but individually (or pray for one another). Note the discipline people said they wanted most to grow in, and pray that God would help them do that. Conclude by asking God to give your group the spirit of service as they practice the disciplines.

TO DO ON YOUR OWN

■ Mathewes-Green warns against overabundance. She fasts to realize her dependence on God. Pray about what you can give up this week to ward against overindulgence. Abstain for a day, a couple of days, or the whole week, then make an effort to tell a fellow group member about how God used your discipline.

■ Take some time during the upcoming week to read and reflect on Frederica Mathewes-Green's article, "Loving the Storm-Drenched" (pages 85–90).

APPENDIX

A NEW KIND OF URBAN CHRISTIAN

Timothy J. Keller

As the city goes, so goes the culture.

In the winter of 2006, two movies mirrored the fractured and confusing relationship between Christians and culture. *The Chronicles of Narnia: The Lion, The Witch and The Wardrobe* struck fear in many secular hearts. Some journalists saw it as an ominous sign of growing right-wing power that a company like Disney would make a movie that had such profound evangelical appeal (and, arguably, content). And why did Disney pull the plug on the gay-friendly TV reality series *Welcome to the Neighborhood*? Isn't this, the pundits asked, what happens when you let Christians influence culture?

At the same time, *The End of the Spear,* the account of five evangelical missionaries martyred in Ecuador, upset some Christians when it was discovered that an active gay man was playing Nate Saint, the lead role in the movie. Conservative cultural commentators were divided. Some, like Eugene Veith of *World* magazine, urged Christians to see the movie and judge it on its artistic merits, not on the morals of its actors off-screen. Others urged a boycott. Major questions about Christianity and culture were raised on hundreds of websites. What makes a movie "Christian"? Do all the actors have to be Christians? If not, which kinds of sinners are allowed, and which are not? Is spiritual compromise inevitable when Christians try to enter mainstream cultural production?

The relationship of Christians to culture is the singular current crisis point for the church. Evangelicals are deeply divided over how to interact with a social order that is growing increasingly post-Christian. Some advise a reemphasis on tradition and on "letting the church be the church," rejecting any direct attempt to influence society as a whole. Others are hostile to culture, but hopeful that they can change it through aggressive action, often of a political sort.

Still others believe that "you change culture one heart at a time." Finally, many are attracted to the new culture and want to reengineer the church to modify its adversarial relationship with culture. Many in the "one heart at a time" party play down doctrine and stress experience, while some in the reengineering group are changing distinctives of evangelical doctrine in the name of cultural engagement. That is fueling much theological controversy, but even people who agree on the need for change disagree over what to *do* to our doctrine to reach the culture.

None of the preceding strategies should be abandoned. We need Christian tradition, Christians in politics, and effective evangelism. And the church has always contextualized itself into its surrounding culture. There are harmful excesses in every approach, however. I think that is because many have turned their specialty into a single magic bullet that will solve the whole problem. I doubt such a magic bullet exists, but just bundling them all together is not sufficient either.

Instead, we need a new and different strategy.

CITY WITHIN A CITY

My first strategic point is simple: *More Christians should live long-term in cities.* Historians point out that by AD 300, the urban populations of the Roman Empire were largely Christian, while the countryside was pagan. (Indeed, the word *pagan* originally meant someone from the countryside—its use as a synonym for a non-Christian dates from this era.) The same was true during the first millennium AD in Europe—the cities were Christian, but the broad population across the countryside was pagan. The lesson from both eras is that when cities are Christian, even if the majority of the population is pagan, society is headed on a Christian trajectory. Why? As the city goes, so goes the culture. Cultural trends tend to be generated in the city and flow outward to the rest of society.

People who live in large urban cultural centers—occupying jobs in the arts, business, academia, publishing, the helping professions, and the media—tend to have a disproportionate impact on how things are done in our culture. Having lived and ministered in New York City for seventeen years, I am continually astonished at how the people I live with and know affect what everyone else in the country sees on the screen, in print, in art, and in business.

I am not talking about the "elite-elites" — the rich and famous — but about the "grassroots-elites." It is not so much the top executives that make MTV what it is, but the scores of young, hip creatives just out of college who take jobs at all levels of the organization. The people who live in cities in the greatest numbers tend to see their values expressed in the culture.

Do I mean that all Christians must live in cities? No. We need Christians and churches everywhere there are people! But I have taken up the call of the late James Montgomery Boice, an urban pastor (at Philadelphia's Tenth Presbyterian Church) who knew that evangelical Christians have been particularly unwilling to live in cities. In his book *Two Cities: Two Loves*, he argued that evangelicals should live in cities in *at least* the same percentage as the general population. If we do not, we should not expect much influence in society.

Once in cities, *Christians should be a dynamic counterculture.* It is not enough for Christians to simply live as individuals in the city. They must live as a particular kind of community. Jesus told his disciples that they were "a city on a hill" that showed God's glory to the world (Matt. 5:14 – 16). Christians are called to be an alternate city within every earthly city, an alternate human culture within every human culture, to show how sex, money, and power can be used in nondestructive ways.

Regarding sex, the alternate city avoids secular society's idolization of sex and traditional society's fear of it. It is a community that so loves and cares for its members that chastity makes sense. It teaches its members to conform their bodily beings to the shape of the gospel — abstinence outside of marriage and fidelity within. Regarding money, the Christian counterculture encourages a radically generous commitment of time, money, relationships, and living space to social justice and the needs of the poor, the immigrant, and the economically and physically weak. Regarding power, Christian community is visibly committed to power-sharing and relationship-building between races and classes that are alienated outside of the body of Christ. The practical evidence of this will be churches that are increasingly multiethnic, both in the congregations at large and in their leadership.

It will not be enough for Christians to form a culture that runs counter to the values of the broader culture. *Christians should be a community radically committed to the good of the city as a whole.* We must move out to sacrificially serve the good of the whole human community, especially the poor. Revelation 21–22 makes it clear that the ultimate purpose of redemption is not to escape the material world, but to renew it. God's purpose is not only saving individuals, but also inaugurating a new world based on justice, peace, and love, not power, strife, and selfishness.

So Christians work for the peace, security, justice, and prosperity of their city and their neighbors, loving them in word and in deed, whether they believe what we do or not. In Jeremiah 29:7, Israel's exiles were called not just to live in the city, but also to love it and work for its *shalom*—its economic, social, and spiritual flourishing. The citizens of God's city are the *best possible* citizens of their earthly cities.

This is the only kind of cultural engagement that will not corrupt us and conform us to the world's pattern of life. If Christians go to urban centers simply to acquire power, they will never achieve cultural influence and change that is deep, lasting, and embraced by the broader society. We must live in the city to serve all the peoples in it, not just our own tribe. We must lose our power to find our (true) power. Christianity will not be attractive enough to win influence except through sacrificial service to all people, regardless of their beliefs.

This strategy (if we must call it that) will work. In every culture, some Christian conduct will be offensive and attacked, but some will be moving and attractive to outsiders. "Though they accuse you— they may see your good deeds and glorify God" (1 Peter 2:12, see also Matt. 5:16). In the Middle East, a Christian sexual ethic makes sense, but not "turn the other cheek." In secular New York City, the Christian teaching on forgiveness and reconciliation is welcome, but our sexual ethics seem horribly regressive. Every non-Christian culture has enough common grace to recognize some of the work of God in the world and to be attracted to it, even while Christianity in other ways will offend the prevailing culture.

So we must neither just denounce the culture nor adopt it. We must sacrificially serve the common good, expecting to be constantly misunderstood and sometimes attacked. We must walk in the steps of the one who laid down his life for his opponents.

THE WORLDVIEW OF WORK

There is another important component to being a Christian counter-culture for the common good. *Christians should be a people who integrate their faith with their work.*

Culture is a set of shared practices, attitudes, values, and beliefs, which are rooted in common understandings of the "big questions" — where life comes from, what life means, who we are, and what is important enough to spend our time doing it in the years allotted to us. No one can live or do their work without some answers to such questions, and every set of answers shapes culture.

Most fields of work today are dominated by a very different set of answers from those of Christianity. But when many Christians enter a vocational field, they either seal off their faith and work like everyone else around them, or they spout Bible verses to their coworkers. We do not know very well how to persuade people of Christianity's answers by showing them the faith-based, worldview roots of *everyone's* work. We do not know how to equip our people to think out the implications of the gospel for art, business, government, journalism, entertainment, and scholarship. Developing humane, creative, and excellent business environments out of our understanding of the gospel can be part of this work. The embodiment of joy, hope, and truth in the arts is also part of this work. If Christians live in major cultural centers in great numbers, doing their work in an excellent but distinctive manner, that alone will produce a different kind of culture than the one in which we live now.

Jewish society sought spiritual power, while Greek society valued wisdom (1 Cor. 1:22–25). Each culture was dominated by a hope that Paul's preaching revealed to be an idol. Yet only in Christ, the true "wisdom of God" for Greeks and the true "power of God" for Jews, could their cultural storylines find a happy ending. The church envisioned in this article attracts people to Christianity by showing how Christ resolves our society's cultural problems and fulfills its cultural hopes. "For the foolishness of God is wiser than man's wisdom, and the weakness of God is stronger than man's strength."

Originally published by The Christian Vision Project in *Christianity Today*, May 2006, vol. 50, no. 5, page 36.

HOW THE KINGDOM COMES

Michael S. Horton

The church becomes countercultural by sinking its roots ever deeper into God's heavenly gifts.

It was confusing to grow up singing both "This World Is Not My Home" and "This Is My Father's World." Those hymns embody two common and seemingly contradictory Christian responses to culture. One sees this world as a wasteland of godlessness, with which the Christian should have as little as possible to do. The other regards cultural transformation as virtually identical to "kingdom activity."

Certainly the answer does not lie in any intrinsic opposition of heaven and earth. After all, Jesus taught us to pray, "Your kingdom come, your will be done on earth as it is in heaven." Rather, the answer is to be sought in understanding the particular moment in redemptive history where God has placed us. We are not yet in the Promised Land, where the kingdom of God may be directly identified with earthly kingdoms and cultural pursuits. Yet we are no longer in Egypt. We are pilgrims in between, on the way.

In Babylon, God commanded the exiles to "build houses and settle down," pursuing the good of their conquering neighbors (Jer. 29). At the same time, he prophesied a new city, an everlasting empire, as the true homeland that would surpass anything Israel had experienced in Canaan.

So both of my childhood hymns tell the truth in their own way: We are pilgrims and strangers in this age, but we "pass through" to the age to come (not some ethereal state of spiritual bliss), which, even now in this present evil age, is dawning.

The challenge is to know what time it is: what the kingdom is, how it comes, and where we should find it right now.

IS CHRISTIANITY A CULTURE?

In the Old Covenant, the kingdom of God was identified with the nation of Israel, anticipating the Last Day by executing on a small scale the judgment and blessings that will come one day to the whole world. Yet Jesus introduced a different polity with the New Covenant. Instead of calling on God's people to drive out the Canaanites in holy war, Jesus pointed out that God blesses both believers and unbelievers. He expects his people to love and serve rather than judge and condemn their neighbors, even their enemies (Matt. 5:43–48; see also Matt. 7:1–6). The wheat and the weeds are to be allowed to grow together, separated only at the final harvest (Matt. 13:24–30). The kingdom at present is hidden under suffering and the cross, conquering through Word and sacrament, yet one day it will be consummated as a kingdom of glory and power. First the cross, weakness, and suffering; then glory, power, and the announcement that the kingdoms of this world have been made the kingdom of Christ (Rev. 11:15; see also Heb. 2:5–18).

So what is the relationship of Christians to culture in this time between the times? Is Jesus Christ Lord over secular powers and principalities? At least in Reformed theology, the answer is yes, though he is Lord in different ways over the world and the church. God presently rules the world through providence and common grace, while he rules the church through Word, sacrament, and covenantal nurture.

This means that there is no difference between Christians and non-Christians with respect to their vocations. "We urge you, brothers, to [love one another] more and more," Paul writes. "Make it your ambition to lead a quiet life, to mind your own business, and to work with your hands, just as we told you, so that your daily life may win the respect of outsiders and so that you will not be dependent on anybody" (1 Thess. 4:10–12). There are no calls in the New Testament either to withdraw into a private ghetto or to "take back" the realms of cultural and political activity. Rather, we find exhortations, like Paul's, to the inauspicious yet crucial task of loving and serving our neighbors with excellence. Until Christ returns, believers will share with unbelievers in pain and pleasure, poverty and wealth, hurricanes and holidays. A believer, however, will not be anxious about the future and will not "grieve like the rest of men, who have no hope," as Paul adds (1 Thess. 4:13), but will be energized in the most mundane daily pursuits by the knowledge that God will raise the dead and set everything right (1 Thess. 4:14–18). We groan inwardly for that final redemption with the whole of creation, precisely because we already have within us the Spirit as a down payment and guarantee (Rom. 8:18–25).

The earthly citizenship to which Jesus, Paul, and Peter referred is therefore a common sphere for believers and unbelievers. The second-century *Epistle to Diognetus* offers a self-portrait of the early Christian community:

> For Christians are distinguished from the rest of men neither by country nor by language nor by customs. For nowhere do they dwell in cities of their own; they do not use any strange form of speech.... But while they dwell in both Greek and barbarian cities, each as his lot was cast, and follow the customs of the land in dress and food and other matters of living, they show forth the remarkable and admittedly strange order of their own citizenship. They live in fatherlands of their own, but as aliens. They share all things as citizens and suffer all things as strangers. Every foreign land is their fatherland, and every fatherland a foreign land.... They pass their days on earth, but they have their citizenship in heaven.

So Christians are not called to make holy apparel, speak an odd dialect of spiritual jargon, or transform their workplace, neighborhood, or nation into the kingdom of Christ. Rather, they are called to belong to a holy commonwealth that is distinct from the regimes of this age (Phil. 3:20–21) and to contribute as citizens and neighbors in temporal affairs. "For here we do not have an enduring city, but we are looking for the city that is to come" (Heb. 13:14). The church, therefore, as the communion of saints gathered by God for preaching, teaching, sacrament, prayer, and fellowship (Acts 2:46–47), is distinct from the broader cultural activities to which Christians are called in love and service to their neighbors. In our day, this pattern is often reversed, creating a pseudo-Christian subculture that fails to take either calling seriously. Instead of being in the world but not of it, we easily become of the world but not in it.

But the church is not really a culture. The kingdom of God is never something that we bring into being, but something that we are receiving. Cultural advances occur by concentrated and collective effort, while the kingdom of God comes to us through baptism, preaching, teaching, Eucharist, prayer, and fellowship. "Therefore, since we are receiving a kingdom that cannot be shaken, let us be thankful, and so worship God acceptably with reverence and awe, for our 'God is a consuming fire'" (Heb. 12:28–29). There is nothing more important for the church than to receive and proclaim the kingdom in joyful assembly, raising children in the covenant of grace. They are heirs with us of that future place for those "who have tasted the heavenly gift, who have shared in the Holy Spirit, who have tasted the goodness of the Word of God and the powers of the coming age" — a holy land which "drinks in the rain often falling on it" and is "farmed" so that it reaps its Sabbath blessing (Heb. 6:4–8).

A COUNTERCULTURE?

If the church is not to be identified with culture, is it necessarily a counterculture? If Christians as well as non-Christians participate in the common curse and common grace of this age in secular affairs, then there is no "Christian politics" or "Christian art" or "Christian literature," any more than there is "Christian plumbing." The church has no authority to bind Christian (much less non-Christian) consciences beyond Scripture. When it does, the church as "counterculture" is really just another subculture, an auxiliary of one faction of the current culture wars, distracted from its proper ministry of witnessing to Christ and the new society that he is forming around himself (Gal. 3:26–29). This new society neither ignores nor is consumed by the cultural conflicts of the day.

Recently, an older pastor told me that during the Vietnam era, two of his parishioners, one a war protestor and the other a veteran, were embroiled in a debate in the parking lot, but then joined each other at the Communion rail with their arms around each other. Here was a witness to the Sabbath rest that awaits us, realizing that we still have, for the time being, vineyards to plant and wars to be for or against as citizens.

Too often, of course, the contemporary church simply mirrors the culture. Increasingly, we are less a holy city drawn together around Christ and more a part of the suburban sprawl that celebrates individual autonomy, choice, entertainment, and pragmatic efficiency. These are values that can build highways and commerce, but they cannot sustain significant bonds across cultural divides and between generations. Capitulating to niche demographics and marketing, churches that once nurtured the young, middle-aged, and elderly together, with all of the indispensable gifts that each one brings to the body of Christ, often now contribute to the rending of this intergenerational fabric. If this is a worrisome trend in the social sphere, it is all the more troubling for a body that is constituted by its Lord as a covenantal community.

To be truly countercultural, the church must first receive and then witness to Peter's claim in Acts 2:39: "The promise is for you and your children and for all who are far off—for all whom the Lord our God will call." The promise is not only for us, but also for our children. According to recent studies by sociologists like Christian Smith, evangelical teens are only slightly less likely than their unchurched friends to adopt a working creed of "moralistic, therapeutic deism." As the diet in our churches is increasingly determined by the spirit of the age, and as youth are treated as borderline cases to be cajoled into thinking God is cool, the church risks abandoning that promise. The "pumped-up" teens in our youth groups today are often tomorrow's skeptics and burnouts. They don't need more hip Christian slogans, T-shirts, and other subcultural distractions, but the means of grace for maturing into coheirs with Christ.

Recently, CNN reporter Anderson Cooper was asked, "Do you think part of your job is to appeal to younger viewers?" "I've never been in a meeting where people said to bring in younger people," he replied. "I think the notion of telling stories differently to appeal to younger people is a mistake. Young people want the same kind of thing older viewers do: interesting, well-told, compelling stories. If you're somehow altering what you're doing because you want to get young viewers, that's a little bit like when your parents go out to buy 'cool' clothes for you." In our culture, relevance is determined—in fact, created—by publicity. But the Word creates its own publicity as it is preached, as the story is told. It creates its own relevance, and as a result, a community that spans the generations.

The promise is not only for us and for our children, Peter says, but "for all who are far off—for all whom the Lord our God will call" (Acts 2:39). And how does he call them? Through the preaching of the gospel. Peter's promise, in fact, is part of such a sermon, proclaiming Christ as the center of Scripture. Refusing to set a covenantal church ("you and your children") against a missional church ("all who are far off"), the apostolic community stuck to its calling and became both an outpost and lightning rod for God's saving activity in the world.

If ours is to truly be a countercultural community, it must begin with the rejection of any notion of self-founding, either in creation or redemption. It is God's choice, not ours; God's "planned community," not ours; God's means of grace, not our ambitious programs, plans, or achievements that extend the kingdom. Being "countercultural" today often amounts to superficial moralism about sex and SUVs, or perhaps creating wholesome novels with Christian heroes, removing offensive language from music lyrics, and encouraging positive values. Beyond that, many of the churches with which I am familiar are captivated by the same obsessions as our culture: religion as individual spirituality, therapy, and sentimentalism. It all serves to keep us turned in on ourselves, like a kid at a carnival instead of a pilgrim en route.

Describing the rapid decline of rural areas that are surrendering to strip malls and homogeneous multinational corporations, Wendell Berry argues, "We must learn to grow like a tree, not like a fire." Berry notes that we are losing our ability to take any place seriously, since this demands patience, love, study, and hard work—in other words, roots. Some use the word "seekers" to describe those we are trying to reach in this culture. But the truth is that they and we are more like tourists than seekers, let alone pilgrims, flying from place to place to consume experiences.

Can churches be a counterculture amidst anonymous neighborhoods and tourist destinations, the apotheoses of individual choice, niche demographics, and marketing? Yes. The church can exist amidst suburban sprawl as easily as in cities or small towns, precisely because its existence is determined by the realities of the age to come—by God's work, rather than by the narrow possibilities of our work in this present age under sin and death. After all, this is our Father's world, even though, for the moment, we are just passing through.

Originally published by The Christian Vision Project in *Christianity Today*, January 2006, vol. 50, no. 1, page 42.

OUR TRANSNATIONAL ANTHEM

Orlando Crespo

O say can you see ... a church where many cultures work together in Christ?

In April 2006, a British producer named Adam Kidron launched a musical volley into the heated American debate over ethnicity and immigration: a new Spanish-language version of the national anthem called *Nuestro Himno*. The song's release provoked condemnation from conservative commentators and a disavowal from President Bush—even though his first presidential campaign frequently featured Spanish-language versions of the anthem. "I think people who want to be a citizen of this country ought to learn English," he said, according to the *New York Times*. "And they ought to learn to sing the national anthem in English."

What do Christians have to contribute to debates like these? The Spanish word *himno* can be translated as *anthem*, but it also can be translated as *hymn*. Is there a uniquely Christian perspective—a Christian hymn, *nuestro himno*—that could serve the common good of a uniquely multiethnic society like America? As the child of Puerto Rican immigrants and as a child of God in Christ, I've become convinced the answer is yes.

GOD'S CREATIVE INTENT

At the core of a biblical understanding of ethnicity is the question of whether ethnicity—the specific and diverse human traditions of culture and language—is a regrettable mistake, an inconsequential accident, or a result of God's creative intent. In recent years, Christians have begun to recover the biblical emphasis on culture. They have looked at the so-called cultural mandate of Genesis 1:28—"fill the earth and subdue it"—and asked whether it could have ever been fulfilled without the accompanying cultural diversity.

As Richard Mouw writes in *When the Kings Come Marching In*, "God intended from the beginning that human beings would 'fill the earth' with the processes, patterns, and products of cultural formation." Kinship groupings would inevitably form as the human race grew in number, along with varying cultural traditions. On the vast earth, with its varied climates and conditions, cultural diversity would flourish naturally, allowing humanity to fulfill God's intent in a variety of ways.

Yet very quickly in Genesis, human culture becomes distorted by the fall. Instead of "filling the earth," people huddle in Babel, where they hatch the plan of building a tower so as not to be "scattered over the face of the whole earth." But this attempt to seek human unity at the expense of filling the earth draws God's intervention. The resulting profusion of languages has often been seen as purely judgment, but it is also grace—the provision of a way to return to God's original plan.

As Randy Woodley writes in his book *Living in Color*, God's intervention at Babel "merely sped up the process of developing the various ethnic groups." To underscore the point, when the Holy Spirit comes upon the first Christians, the miracle is not that they speak the same language—rather, those gathered at Pentecost each hear the mighty works of God being declared in their *own* language. The barrier to human communication imposed by God at Babel is removed at Pentecost, but the glorious diversity of human culture is blessed.

When Christians seek to be "colorblind"—a word that suggests that ethnic distinctions are ultimately irrelevant—they unknowingly imitate the tower-builders' fear of diversity. In practice, colorblindness usually means persons from minority cultures allow their cultural distinctiveness to become invisible, while persons from the majority culture expect others to adapt to their culture. A colorblind church is unable to appreciate the amazing cultural diversity to which God brings salvation: "You are worthy to take the scroll and to open its seals," the elders sing to the Lamb. "Because you were slain, and with your blood you purchased for God members of every tribe and language and people and nation" (Rev. 5:9 TNIV).

If God begins with a cultural mandate for us to fill the earth, doing so by means of the rich diversity of ethnicities and cultures, and if Scripture ends with all ethnic groups worshiping God, then living a vibrant ethnic life in the here and now is something deeply blessed by God. What are the practical steps we can take toward a life that blesses and affirms cultural diversity?

THE COURAGE TO BE DIFFERENT

For many of us who are ethnic minorities, the first step is having the courage to live out the fullness of our ethnic identity. When I was seven years old, my family became the first Puerto Ricans to move into a white neighborhood. We endured taunting from the family directly across the street, as well as racial insults based on our Latino heritage. It was all too easy to learn the lesson that being Puerto Rican was dirty and unacceptable. Bigotry and racism left an indelible mark on my soul.

But as I studied Scripture, I observed God working through the ethnicities and cultures of prominent figures like Moses (a tri-cultural person, Hebrew-Egyptian-Midianite!), Mordecai and Esther (Persian Israelites), and Paul (a Jewish Roman citizen). For each of them, their ethnic identity was central to God's plan for the deliverance of his people. If any of them had chosen to simply assimilate to the dominant culture, they would have missed God's deepest purposes for them. I began to believe that God could have a purpose for my ethnic identity—that my Latino identity was not an accident or a mistake, but a gift.

I discovered when I had trouble praying in English, my heart language of Spanish helped me overcome spiritual stagnation. The Latino value of *fiesta*—celebrating life even in the midst of pain—helped me hold onto my faith in difficult times. The closeness of my Puerto Rican family gave me a window into the love of my Father in heaven. I started to see that my bilingual abilities gave me opportunities for ministry, especially among second-generation Latino youth, who were trying to straddle two very different cultural worlds.

As I grew in confidence in my ethnic identity, I was able to bring elements of my Latino culture, like our great capacity for hospitality, into the work of the predominantly white organization where I served in ministry.

Five years ago, I left a job I very much loved, codirecting InterVarsity Christian Fellowship's ministry in New York City, to take on a role that had never existed before—as the first national director of LaFe,

73

InterVarsity's Latino ministry. This decision has brought out gifts in me, and in others in our organization, that would not have been discovered otherwise. In five years, we have grown from nineteen Latino campus ministers to forty-five across the country. Of the 32,000 students InterVarsity works with in the U.S., 913 are Latino, a 21 percent increase over the last five years.

THE COURAGE TO BE WHITE

Whites, too, have something to contribute to a uniquely Christian approach to ethnic identity. In InterVarsity, we are learning that it is not enough for our ethnic minority campus ministers to see their ethnicity as a blessing. It is also vital that our white campus ministers live out of the beauty and strengths of their ethnicity. The first step for them is simply to recognize that they have a God-given ethnic identity—that being white is not just neutral or "normal," but a particular cultural heritage that can be redeemed and used for good.

White identity is invisible until it engages actively with other cultures and discovers what other cultures are reacting to and why. So it is essential for whites to enter into real relationships and partnerships with nonwhites, even to the point of feeling out of place.

As our white staff have pursued such partnerships, they have developed a new and deeper sense of their white identity and a greater commitment to stay engaged in difficult issues of race. They are also being set free from a common affliction of whites who have become aware of the history of white privilege in America: immobilization by shame, guilt, or apathy.

One result of this process in InterVarsity has been Paula Harris and Doug Schaupp's book, *Being White: Finding Our Place in a Multiethnic World*. Paula and Doug identify some of the unique gifts and values of white culture, including the inherent worth of the individual, the importance of self-determination, and the commitment to take risks and solve problems.

THE COURAGE TO WORK TOGETHER

In *Living in Color*, Randy Woodley, a Native American, gives a powerful account of what cultural partnerships can accomplish in addressing social issues. The state of Montana wanted, in the interests of safety and economic growth, to expand Highway 93, which ran through beautiful land in the Flathead Indian Reservation. The Salish and Kootenai tribes, however, were concerned that such an expansion would destroy wildlife, bring in new development, and eventually lead to unsustainable population growth.

As these two ethnic groups worked with the majority culture, they created a plan. They would build a four-lane highway that would respect the land and its inhabitants, following the natural contours of the land and including 42 wildlife crossings under and over the highway. In the end, not only did this design honor the tribes' concern for respect for land and animals, it actually made the highway safer, furthering the state's original purpose.

The two Native American tribes sought to protect the land, while the Montana Department of Transportation, representing white culture, placed great value on safety and economic growth (by expanding job opportunities through tourism). The priorities of each culture ended up serving the common good of the others.

NUESTRO HIMNO

Can the church, with its unique reach into nearly every "tribe and language and people and nation" represented in the United States, become a model of this kind of partnership? What might our song, *nuestro himno*, contribute to vexed questions about ethnicity in America?

In the case of the national anthem, Christians could begin by observing that Pentecost affirms the value of every culture and language. So when Latino citizens sing the national anthem in Spanish, we understand that they are embracing their bicultural and bilingual American Latino identity. They are singing about the nation they love in the language that resonates in their soul.

At the same time, Latino Christians understand that the national anthem is an important cultural icon in its original language—a key part of white American culture. No translation of our treasured anthem should be a replacement for it. So we could well agree with President Bush that every citizen, including Latino citizens, should also be able to sing the national anthem in English.

Finally, we might recognize that the national anthem is translated into myriad tongues every day. It is impossible for someone dominant in a language other than English not to translate a song like the national anthem in his or her head. Furthermore, the national anthem has already been translated into Spanish a number of times during the past hundred years, and until recently, this was not politically controversial. The question for our time might become who should do an official translation that would do justice to the original text but also free an important group of citizens to hear and sing the text's original meaning in their own language.

A VITAL PURPOSE

Whatever happens with the national anthem, my hope is that the church in America will embrace its ethnic diversity as a vital part of humanity that can be redeemed for the purposes of God. If we do, we can offer something special to the wider world.

We are beginning to understand that racial healing is one purpose of the church, tearing down the walls that still separate us as brothers and sisters in Christ. May Jesus' prayer to the Father for us be answered in our generation: "I pray ... that all of them may be one, Father, just as you are in me and I am in you. May they also be in us so that the world may believe ... that you sent me and have loved them even as you have loved me" (John 17:20–23). That, indeed, is *nuestro himno*.

Originally published by The Christian Vision Project in *Christianity Today*, August 2006, vol. 50, no. 8, page 32.

MEEKS PREACHES CHURCH ACTIVISM

Mick Dumke

At the Rainbow/PUSH Coalition's annual convention in July [2000], the Rev. James T. Meeks encouraged churches to get involved in community revitalization by buying neighborhood grocery stores, restaurants and franchises for McDonald's or Krispy Kreme Doughnuts.

"An old song goes 'I'd rather have Jesus than silver and gold.' Well, since it's a song about choices, I'd rather have both," Meeks said to the clergy and others gathered at the convention. "There is no law that the neighborhood grocery store has to be owned by foreigners."

Meeks, the executive vice president of Rainbow/PUSH, has frequently led his own congregation—the 12,000-member Salem Baptist Church of Chicago, 11816 S. Indiana Avenue—into community and political activism.

In 1998, he led a successful drive for a referendum prohibiting the sale of alcohol in parts of the Roseland neighborhood. Mayor Richard M. Daley attended a March 19 press conference at Meeks' church in support of similar vote-dry campaigns.

The following year, Meeks endorsed Salem member Anthony Beale in his winning bid to become the 9th Ward alderman.

Salem currently owns and operates the 11,000 square-foot House of Peace bookstore, at 11500 S. Michigan Avenue, and runs a school, Salem Christian Academy.

"Politics does not make one religious, but religion makes one political," Meeks said in an interview.

He criticized the Daley administration for lagging in its minority hiring, but said overall Daley "has been a good mayor."

Beale, he added, should forge close ties with city hall. "You don't get [services] delivered to your ward by making yourself the mayor's chief opponent," Meeks said. "I'd hope he would stand with the mayor when he's right and stand against him when he's wrong."

According to city records, in 1995 the city's Department of Human Services awarded Salem Baptist Church of Chicago a Community Development Block Grant worth up to $12,500. Salem was paid a total of $11,270 in city payments from 1992 to 1996, mostly from the human services department.

But Meeks said that his church has never received any special treatment from the Daley administration. "We have never received anything free from the city—not a vacant lot, not a parking lot," he said. "And I wasn't always huge. This church started with 200 people, and we never took anything."

Meeks is now planning to develop affordable housing and said the church tried to acquire land through the city's Department of Planning. But the process took so long that Salem decided to purchase a vacant block on its own. "If the city does it on the next block, that's fine, too," he said.

Meeks denied his relationship with the city compromised his independence, saying he and the mayor "don't play golf or tennis together."

And because elected officials increasingly depend on churches to provide social services, clergy can remain free of political pressures, he said. "The government is in need of faith-based organizations who know communities, who can be trusted to do the right thing. Who else does the government give the money to? The gangs?

"There are no other well-disciplined, well-organized groups in the country that know the communities, except the church," Meeks said. "It's got to be them."

Used by permission of *The Chicago Reporter.* "Meeks Preaches Church Activism," by Mick Dumke, Copyright © October 2000. http://www.chicagoreporter.com/2000/10–2000/op-ed/meeks.htm.

HABITS OF HIGHLY EFFECTIVE JUSTICE WORKERS

Rodolpho Carrasco

Should we protest the system or invest in a life? Yes.

Sixteen years ago, I took my undergraduate degree and headed straight to the 'hood. Since then, I've lived one block from the corner of Howard and Navarro in Pasadena, an area that once had the highest daytime crime rate in Southern California. I've lived through the 1992 Rodney King riots, the 1996 welfare-reform bill, and the rise of compassionate conservatism. And I've lived through a small revolution in how Christians think about justice.

Not so long ago, evangelical Christians who served the poor often found themselves on the defensive among fellow believers. Now it's the rare church that doesn't engage in works of mercy and justice. Watching this evangelical wave of concern and action, I've been greatly encouraged. Yet as I listen to my fellow justice-impassioned Christ-followers, whether they are newbies or grizzled veterans, I often hear only part of the message of justice.

There is no shortage of protest across the political spectrum. Some promote fair trade over free trade and argue for turning the minimum wage into a living wage; they seek to strengthen immigrant rights and oppose racism. Others object to activist judges, family-hostile state laws and school curricula, and porous borders. But increasingly, all these concerns are framed in terms of concern for the most vulnerable members of society. These issues rouse people out of their living rooms, out of the pews, and into society to work for change.

While I celebrate this development, I worry that we are perilously weak at walking alongside the poor, at investing directly into the lives of individuals to give them what they truly need—not what we believe they need or what our policy statements tell us they need.

I've found that it's relatively easy to raise a voice in protest, but unfathomably hard to invest in a life.

JUSTICE HABITS

Growing up, I had to learn how to manage money, how to be a good employee, how to act in someone else's house, how to study, and how to delay gratification. As an orphan in a poor East Los Angeles neighborhood, learning these things was a matter of life and death.

My mother died when I was six. My father had already left us. My sister, twenty years old at the time, became mother, father, grandma, and grandpa for my other two siblings and me. She drilled those basic life skills into me. Alongside her were members of a small Baptist church who taught us the Scriptures, teachers who saw the potential in the Carrasco kids, and employers who held us accountable for our behavior on the job.

Years later, the Carrasco family had emerged from poverty, and I had a bachelor's degree from Stanford. I went straight to northwest Pasadena to join Harambee Ministries and be a part of breaking the cycle of poverty. I initially assumed that youth in the community surrounding Harambee were learning what I had learned growing up. And some were. Others, however—many others—were failing to learn these most basic skills.

Take money skills. While some urban youth have a good grasp of personal finance, many don't. How to manage a credit card, why to avoid check-cashing shops, why a good credit report is a critical tool in America—most youth on my street know almost nothing about these topics.

Those who lack knowledge and experience managing money must be taught. But here is where doing justice by investing in the personal development of the poor gets hard.

Imagine teaching a young adult male how to manage a salary that provides for housing, food, family expenses, transportation, and emergencies. He might complete a class at a church or community center. But will that information stick? Money management must be practiced in order to be truly learned. Is this young man getting the training he needs? More often than not, the answer is no, especially among fatherless young men. The older he is, the more bad habits he is likely to have accrued over the years. While he painstakingly unlearns those habits, he still has to make ends meet.

After seeing this pattern repeatedly in northwest Pasadena, I began to wonder where I learned about money. After all, at age six I was the at-risk poster child. I was "the poor." But my sister was a math major—and that fact alone made a difference. When I was in fifth grade, she made me multiply the number of chores I had done by ten cents to arrive at my weekly "salary." At various stages of my life, she instructed, cajoled, and held me accountable. One year, she gave me $4,000 and suggested I take up day trading. By prodding me to save, plan, and experiment, she helped me learn. It took years.

Then there came a day, as a young adult, when the problem was not understanding, but confidence. Deep down, I didn't believe I could really hold on to money, that this particular Mexican would ever rise above his circumstances. I went through a severe crisis of self-doubt.

I had a lot of support from family and friends, yet it took a long time to learn what I know now about finances. Now add issues like education, employment, and marriage. There is no way around these basic life skills if a person is ever to escape poverty. The investment needed is long, sacrificial, and, frankly, tedious. Doing justice by walking alongside people as they develop critical life skills is not exciting. Protesting on Wall Street against globalization is exciting. Getting arrested at the courthouse is exciting. Filling the National Mall with hundreds of thousands of people is exciting. But staying proximate to people as they learn lessons they should have learned years ago? When's the last time you saw that on CNN?

THE DIGNITY OF ACCOUNTABILITY

It's not just justice workers who need to accept responsibility for investing in the skills of the poor. The poor themselves must realize their capacity to overcome poverty.

In saying this, I'm not blaming the victim and letting powerful people and systemic powers off the hook. I mean nothing of the sort. What I'm getting at is something I learned from Harambee's founder, John Perkins.

If you are down and out, Perkins would ask, are you going to sit back and wait for someone else to transform your situation? Are you going to rely on the very government, for example, that has failed you? Your best chance is to take responsibility for changing your circumstances. Yes, you will need support from others and policies shaped by protesters for justice, but you are the principal engine for change in your own life.

I believe that, for every person is created in God's image. The same God who created the world *ex nihilo* has created us capable of great things. We are able, because he is able. Because our dignity comes directly from God, it is not only possible for people to rise above their conditions — it should be expected.

Yet it took a disappointment for me to learn just how hard it is to put that theology into practice.

One teen we'd known since elementary school had a father who was nowhere to be found and a mother who struggled to raise him and his siblings. By his teen years, street vice had become attractive. We at Harambee intervened, drawing him into our lives and our programs. After he graduated from high school, we helped him find a job — a great job, in fact.

Then he got fired. The reasons weren't complicated: He ignored rules, was often late for work, and was oblivious to his employer's wishes.

Gradually, I realized where this young man had learned much of his poor work ethic: on our staff. I wanted him to stay close to our community and off the streets, so I made concessions when I felt that discipline might turn him away from us.

This young man was now another unemployed urban male. Seeing him on the street, the protester against injustice might easily surmise that racism, discrimination, a bad economy, or any number of social factors had made this young man a victim. But I knew differently. His circumstance wasn't the result of injustice, but of a flaw in his work ethic, a flaw that could have been corrected.

Yes, my role in this young man's drama was secondary. The primary responsibility lay with his own choices. But he was close to me for some time, and I failed to use the myriad opportunities I had to shape his character. I meant well, but I turned out to be part of the reason he found himself unemployed and broke a year out of high school.

Since then, we've revamped our youth jobs program. We've made it harder for students to get in. Once in, we work them, as we say in the 'hood, like they stole something. We expect a lot from them. A new teen at Harambee has to demonstrate high character immediately, because many little children in our after-school program are watching everything these teenagers do.

It's a lot of pressure on the teens, but they rise to the occasion—or they get the boot. Our present crop has a high work ethic, and I feel hopeful they will be very employable very soon. Even those we've given the boot to are stepping up in their responsibilities. I heard the other day that one recent high school graduate is working at Starbucks, getting solid hours, and learning the ropes. He's been there for four months, and his employment future looks promising.

GET CLOSER

When did you last spend time with a poor person, an at-risk individual, or someone in need? When was the last time you were close to them for an extended period? I ask, because that's what Jesus did. He was close to the poor who needed justice. The Messiah was sent to preach good news to the poor, to proclaim freedom for prisoners, recovery of sight for the blind, release for the oppressed, and the arrival of the Jubilee year (Luke 4:18–19). He did this first by becoming incarnate, one of us. He did not commute from heaven in a fiery chariot. "The Word became flesh," says John, "and made his dwelling among us."

In urban ministry circles, we call this relocation. Many urban ministers intentionally live in the neighborhoods they seek to serve. Proximity builds trust with neighbors, especially if a racial divide must be crossed. Relocation also helps urban ministers discern the roots of need. A man may ask me every day for money. He's down and out, he says. But if I live in that community, I'll be able to discern if he is down and out because of systemic injustice or because he does not want to work. Then I'll be able to share with him what he truly needs.

People in need of justice are not just in the inner city. Individuals and families are struggling in suburban and rural settings as well. In many cases, you do not need to relocate in order to meet a need. But when working for justice, it is crucial to have personal proximity to injustice.

Up close, the protest-oriented injustice-fighter may discover that some matters are best settled by a personal intervention, not a new law. The personal-responsibility injustice-fighter may discover that impersonal systems often devastate the lives of the poor, and that these systems must indeed be protested.

In either case, the best way to get closer to doing justice for the poor is, quite simply, to get closer.

Originally published by The Christian Vision Project in *Christianity Today*, February 2006, vol. 50, no. 2, page 46.

LOVING THE STORM-DRENCHED

Frederica Mathewes-Green

We can no more change the culture than we can the weather. Fortunately, we've got more important things to do.

If you hang around with Christians, you find that the same topic keeps coming up in conversation: their worries about "the culture." Christians talk about sex and violence in popular entertainment. They talk about bias in news reporting. They talk about how their views are ignored or misrepresented. "The culture" appears to be an aggressive challenger to "the church," and Christians keep worrying what to do about it. You soon get the impression that Church Inc. and Culture Amalgamated are like two corporations confronting each other at a negotiating table. Over there sits Culture — huge, complex, and self-absorbed. It's powerful, dangerous, unpredictable, and turbulent. Church is smaller, anxious; it studies Culture, trying to figure out a way to weasel in.

But there are flaws in this picture. For one thing, neither party is as monolithic as it seems. There are many devout believers among the ranks of journalists and entertainers, and there are even more culture-consumers among the ranks of devout believers. Indeed, it's almost impossible to avoid absorbing this culture; if you sealed the windows, it would leak in under the door. I once heard a retreat leader say she'd attempted a "media fast," but found the gaudy world met her on every side. "I may be free in many ways," she said, "but I am not free to not know what Madonna is doing."

Furthermore, the church is not a corporation; rather, it is incorporate, or better, incarnate, carried in the vulnerable bodies of fallible individuals who love and follow Jesus Christ. The culture is even less of an organization. It is more like a photomosaic composed of tiny faces, faces of the millions of people — or billions, rather, thanks to the worldwide toxic leak of American entertainment—who are caught up in its path.

The influence of the culture on all those individuals, including Christians, is less like that of a formal institution and more like the weather. We can observe that, under current conditions, it's cloudy with a chance of cynicism. Crudity is up, nudity is holding steady, and there is a 60 percent chance that any recent movie will include a shot of a man urinating. Large fluffy clouds of sentimental spirituality are increasing on the horizon, but we have yet to see whether they will blow toward or away from Christian truth. Stay tuned for further developments.

As Mark Twain famously remarked, everyone talks about the weather, but no one does anything about it. I think much of our frustration is due to trying to steer the weather, rather than trying to reach individuals caught up in the storm.

It's possible to influence weather within limits, to seed clouds for rain, for example. And it is right for us to consider what we can do to provide quality fiction, films, and music, and to prepare young Christians to work in those fields. We can do some things to help improve ongoing conditions. But it is futile to think that we will one day take over the culture and steer it. It's too ungainly. It is composed of hundreds of competing sources. No one controls it.

What's more, it is already changing—constantly, ceaselessly, seamlessly—changing whether we want it to or not, in ways we can't predict, much less control. If you take the cultural temperature at any given moment, you will find that some of the bad things are starting to fade, and improvement is beginning to appear; simultaneously, some good things are starting to fall out of place, and a new bad thing is emerging.

Not only can we not control this process, we can't even perceive it until changes are so far developed as to be entrenched. Chasing the culture is a way to guarantee that you will always be a step behind the times.

WAITING FOR FUN TO HURT

One of my favorite classic films is *It Happened One Night* (1934), starring Clark Gable and Claudette Colbert. This comedy won five

Academy Awards and deserved them; it has some of the most original characters and clever writing you'll find in any American film. The underlying premise is that a couple will not have sex before marriage, and this romantic tension drives the plot.

Yet that does not guarantee uniform "positive values." Everyone in the movie smokes, including the heroine (while wearing her wedding gown). It's not even safe smoking: We see the hero light up in a haystack. What's more, the hero regularly directs physical threats at the heroine; he says, for example, "She needs someone to take a sock at her once a day, whether she's got it coming to her or not." While the cultural barometer in recent decades has been falling on sexual morality, indicators for smoking and violence against women have indisputably improved.

But the most striking element is the attitude toward drunkenness. The first time we see Gable's character he is roaring drunk, and this is assumed to be hilarious. His drunkenness is encouraged and subsidized by other characters. In the post-Prohibition decades, being drunk (as opposed to merely drinking) was seen as rebellious, cool, and fashionable, and people who objected were depicted as prudes and squares. That fad eventually passed, when the damage done by alcoholism could no longer be romanticized away.

Now, in the post-sexual-revolution decades, being promiscuous is seen as rebellious, cool, and fashionable, and people who object are depicted as prudes and squares. That fad will eventually pass, too, when the damage done by abortion, divorce, and sexually transmitted diseases can no longer be romanticized away.

We cannot instigate this change by appealing to morality, but simple common sense has a stubborn tendency to reemerge. By the '70s it was becoming apparent that alcoholism dealt too much disease, divorce, and family disintegration to be all that funny. This change was not achieved by the Woman's Christian Temperance Union (WCTU) finally coming up with the bulls-eye slogan that would "change hearts and minds." Instead, people just came to their senses.

But note that when the WCTU is mentioned today, it's still seen as a bastion of prudes and squares. They were not vindicated, even though they turned out to be right. And it may be the same with us. We may always be seen as prudes and squares. Despite this, sexual common sense is likely to reemerge. (It happened once before:

Films of the 1920s through 1950s reflect an acceptance of male adultery that would be horrifying today. We presume that these old movies will showcase "old-fashioned values," and they do; we just don't realize what those values were.) So sometimes cultures shift for the better. When so-called fun hurts enough, people stop doing it.

THE POUNDING STORM

The culture, then, is like the weather. We may be able to influence it in modest ways, seeding the clouds, but it is a recipe for frustration to expect that we can direct it. Nor should we expect positive change without some simultaneous downturn in a different corner. Nor should we expect that any change will be permanent. The culture will always be shifting, and it will always be with us.

God has not called us to change the weather. Our primary task as believers, and our best hope for lasting success, is to care for individuals caught up in the pounding storm. They are trying to make sense of their lives with inadequate resources, confused and misled by the Evil One and unable to tell their left hand from their right (Jonah 4:11). They are not a united force; they are not even in solidarity with each other, apart from the unhappy solidarity of being molded by the same junk-food entertainment. They are sheep without a shepherd, harassed and helpless (Matt. 9:36). Only from a spot of grounded safety can anyone discern what to approve and what to reject in the common culture.

But we must regretfully acknowledge that we, too, are shaped by the weather in ways we do not realize. Most worryingly, it has induced us to think that the public square is real life. We are preoccupied with that external world, when our Lord's warnings have much more to do with our intimate personal lives, down to the level of our thoughts.

So, when Christians gather, there's less talk about humility, patience, and the struggle against sin. Instead, there's near-obsessive emphasis on the need for a silver-bullet media product that will magically open the nation to faith in Jesus Christ. Usually, the product they crave is a movie. Now, I'm delighted that Christians are working in Hollywood; we should be salt and light in every community that exists, and so powerful a medium clearly merits our powerful stories. But it's telling that the media extravaganza so eagerly awaited is not a novel or a song, something an individual might undertake, but a movie: something that will require enormous physical and professional resources, millions of dollars, and, basically, work done by somebody else.

This focus on an external, public sign is contrary to the embodied mission of the church. Christ planned to attract people to himself through the transformed lives of his people. It's understandable that we feel chafed by what media giants say about us and the things we care about, and that we crave the chance to tell our own side of the story. It's as if the world's ballpark is ringed with billboards, and we rankle because we should have a billboard too. But if someone should actually see our billboard, and be intrigued, and walk in the door of a church, he would find that he had joined a community that was just creating another billboard.

A COMMON ENEMY

One excellent way to see how much our culture's passing weather patterns have influenced us is to read old books. If you receive all your information from contemporary writers, Christian or secular, you will never perceive whole concepts that people in other generations could see. (For example, earlier generations of Christians perceived a power in sexual purity that eludes us completely; we can only fall back on "don'ts.") Every Christian should always have at his bedside at least one book that is at least fifty years old—the older the better.

Sure, you can make yourself read the contemporary magazines and authors you disagree with, but even they share the same underlying assumptions. It's as if we see our "culture war" opponents standing on the cold peak of an iceberg. From our corresponding peak, all we can discern between us is an expanse of dark water. But underneath that water, the two peaks are joined in a single mass. The common assumptions we share are invisible to us, but they will be perceived, and questioned, by our grandchildren.

C. S. Lewis has a wonderful passage on this phenomenon in his introduction to Athanasius's *On the Incarnation*: "Every age has its own outlook. It is specially good at seeing certain truths and specially liable to make certain mistakes. We all, therefore, need the books that will correct the characteristic mistakes of our own period. And that means the old books."

The "old books" can help us discern the prevailing assumptions of our cultural moment, not only concerning the content of our discussions, but also their style. We expect that combatants will be casual, rather than formal. We expect that their arguments will be illustrated by popular culture, rather than the classics or history. Conservatives and liberals agree that it is admirable to be rebellious and challenge authority, and both sides are at pains to present the other side as authority.

More serious, however, is a tone of voice we adopt from the culture: sarcastic, smart-alecky, jabbing, and self-righteous. We feel the sting of such treatment and give it right back; we feel anger or even wounded hatred toward those on the "other side." But God does not hate them; he loves them so much he sent his Son to die for them. We are told to pray for those who persecute us and to love our enemies. The weight of antagonistic and mocking big-media machinery is the closest thing we've got for practicing that difficult spiritual discipline. If we really love these enemies, we will want the best for them, the very best thing we have, which is the knowledge and love of God.

Smart-alecky speech doesn't even work. It may win applause, but it does not win hearts. It hardens the person who feels targeted, because he feels mocked and misrepresented. It increases bad feeling and anger. No one changed his mind on an issue because he was humiliated into it. In fact, we are misguided even to think of our opponents in the "culture wars" as enemies in the first place. They are not our enemies, but hostages of the Enemy. We have a common Enemy who seeks to destroy us both, by locking them in confusion and by luring us to self-righteous pomposity.

Culture is not a monolithic power we must defeat. It is the battering weather conditions that people, harassed and helpless, endure. We are sent out into the storm like a St. Bernard with a keg around our neck, to comfort, reach, and rescue those who are thirsting, most of all, for Jesus Christ.

Originally published by The Christian Vision Project in *Christianity Today*, March 2006, vol. 50, no. 3, page 36.

APPENDIX 6

We want to hear from you. Please send your comments about this book to us in care of zreview@zondervan.com. Thank you.

ZONDERVAN.com/
AUTHORTRACKER
follow your favorite authors